the

merino

princess

the merino princess

selected poems

bernadette hall

victoria
university
press

VICTORIA UNIVERSITY PRESS
Victoria University of Wellington
PO Box 600 Wellington
www.vuw.ac.nz/vup

First published 2004

National Library of New Zealand Cataloguing-in-Publication Data

Hall, Bernadette.
Merino Princess : selected poems / Bernadette Hall.
ISBN 0-86473-492-1
I. Title.
NZ821.2—dc 22

Published with the assistance of a grant from

ARTS COUNCIL OF NEW ZEALAND *TOI AOTEAROA*

Printed by Astra Print

contents

from

heartwood

lacework

The poems must be of metal;
Etruscan iron cut clean, sharp,
tough as the lacework on the verandah
at Dundas Street bristling with mosses,
cobbled webs, bird shit, rust enough;
thrusting bright chunks of hills, of sky,
into my narrowed eyes; holding up my roof.

pansies

my mother
when
my father
died

dried
the tawny
fronds of
her sorrow

&
stored them
in silence

that summer
I planted
pansies

all round
the house
a moat of petals

even now
my mother
speaks of
my father

in
directly

praising
the petals
of pansies

looking back

for Jan Devereux

an exotic bird
in expensive drab

you dare still
beautiful as Bowie

frayed hands wired
with silver & gold

always did have style.
in glass towers

before the Fall
we honed our deadly

virtues sharp as sticks:
& were they married

in the eyes of God?
(as big as soup plates)

& no meat ever
on Fridays.

we bled outside
the holy of holies.

towers topple:
your old man

buggered off to Aus.
mine said he was immortal

but he lied.
trees were taller then

the river wider
& full of sun

barefoot I'd run
on gravel

faster
than any boy

& called
myself Joe.

iconoclast

Very tricksy are the Irish
aunts, adroit at half-truths,

needing a tragedy for definition.
No one spins it quite as they,

gold from straw. Sometimes
they look at me, unsure, as if

I might say. And Eleanor jumped
from a bridge which alters most

things. Sharp as tin, the women
slipstitch outward signs to

fine linen; shuffle inner grace;
thumb rainbeads on fibre-optic

trees; rub crumbs for sparrows.
Uncomforted, in baleen clouds

I see the subtle shades of avalanches.
I wave her name like a white flag.

Not knowing the god language,
I learn these things off

by my heart. Pulling down icons,
find I love them as they fall.

on hearing of the death
of the civil rights lawyer
Victoria Mxenge, murdered
in South Africa, August 1985

Juliet has lost a hooked milk tooth,
stashes it with petals in a jar.

So many losses, and not last this least,
a syllable in our litany of grief.

The estuary flows black
as the carved lips of the women.

And the sky too
round the white heel of the moon.

There should be music
and I as beautiful as the dancer.

holà! holà!
elle sanglote, la mer

amica

for Joanna Margaret Paul

The house is a reliquary
of insects, flowers & fingernails
& this is rare, Amica, that you assume
with your Etruscan air its essence;
lying on the hill arch of your arm;
on a sarcophagus. Someone is whistling
in the kitchen, laying down new territory
with aluminium brightness. All the windows
are open. Ivory tides wash out, wash in
& you sing the mysteries: that love
is a gift; that nothing is ever lost;
that death is the centre of a long life.

for my catholic mother

Truly you are brave
full of faith & graceful

laying your hands on the body
of the house. I'd like to light

a holy roman candle for you
which is better than a poke

in the eye with a burnt stick
& polish up your batik face

a bit. Godblessed & all
the rest of it, lean on me,

lady, with your protestant leg.
We'll make the cat laugh yet.

from

of
elephants
etc

ritual for a white rabbit

I cut a grave precisely
in blue clay   he curls

like a cashew there
in a white lace pillowcase

who poured himself
like milk through green

weeds   whiter than my finger
tip bleached by elastoplast

he found sex simple & death
he had no expectations

his gift was gentleness

# of elephants etc

i.

I planted a tree hip high
now it shelters my children

a luminous cloak of white
fire & bees short-circuit

my hand on the elephant skin
where blossoms break through

like bubbles of blood

once in a film I saw an elephant
dying whom young bulls mounted

gently & in turn to ripen
her womb for the new season

but failed to hold her back

ii.

perhaps it is most like this
to die   to enter the possibility

of a poem   the lean silence
of dry hills that hold us

like clear bowls of water

in the picture

for Michael Harlow

In the picture, I am leading you
through the darker rooms of the house
& someone in a blue floral dress flings
her arms wide. She is very angry
under her straw hat.

                 Angels like Giotto's
hang upside down from heaven. They are
swart & surly in white boiler-suits &
gumboots. They waver in a low wattage.
And there I am again

                    in the doorway
of a wrecked train. An orange thread slips
like a garrotte, it's flame & all the angels
yelling 'Jump!' I hunker down & lift
a listening face.

                It is always too late.

mayday

The flannel hills fade out
fade in, perfecting it,

to the rapturous clapping of rain.
A stagy day, illuminant.

The windows fill with leaves.
I am teased out like rough wool.

The man in the truck
has a rifle across his knees.

A hint of snow.

mills & boon

Three years I am obsessed
with him, the man

who is not my husband.
Shivered, burned,

no joking, truly I did burn
& dreamt him dead.

Black gloves, a beret
on the coffin & hooded

outlaws firing a salute.
I too would have walked

out in a hail of bullets,
slap in the middle of a cliché.

But said nothing.
Just sat in Irish silence

for three years on his beach.
Brittle with bitterness,

I prayed for him.
He would come, hold me,

fold me in an old tweed
coat, stand equal naked

in the gleaming surf,
the night all sparrow colours,

golden fur down the black
spine of the headland

& moth embroideries.

The imagery made me,
makes me weep.

I was completely fictional.

Then one day it dawned
in a flurry of birdsong

& white camellia
cloud & blue & blue

& the tug of a green
cricket in my glass hand.

I am the writer
of the script.

Barefaced, with armfuls
of awful facts, I turned,

turn each new leaf,
my eye on a stunning ending.

I have almost forgotten his name.

windsurfing

the hills are drawing
a fine line of it

like my mouth when I'm saintly

pines clump over there
like the hairs on my strong

right arm   the choices
are always the same

for a mercenary   for a monk.

hung   a bright moth
on the thin lake skin

slicing a grin

I'm still at odd angles
laid out   on shifting air

hanging onto an idea.

bowl

for Viv Holmes

i.

You carry the bowl around
in your head till one day
the block jolts.
                    You press
the grain against the lathe,
fiercely, gently. The bowl
is well aware of its own
shape,
            a hemisphere of honey
light, flawed to perfection.
You go back & back to the same
leaping off place.

ii.

                        Falling in love
is a 'genetically instinctual
component of mating behaviour'.
Falling in love is shapelessness,
a collapse of boundaries.
                        The bowl
takes a bite out of the white
window frame.
                It has shed the grand
& shaggy gestures of a tree. Compact
now, it pulls itself together,
alert, passionate, reticent.

iii.

        Miracles are a matter
of timing, grace is routine.
Run your fingers on the lip
of the bowl, round & round
without end.
        Gradually
you will come to the place
where you know what you are doing.

mr & mrs bach

it must be
that he loved

& she
though ages apart

& twenty-one children
you can hear it

in the breathy flute
the clean hit on the neck

of the violin
dithering

like white moths
in feathered grass

ending always
mouth to mouth

from

the
persistent
levitator

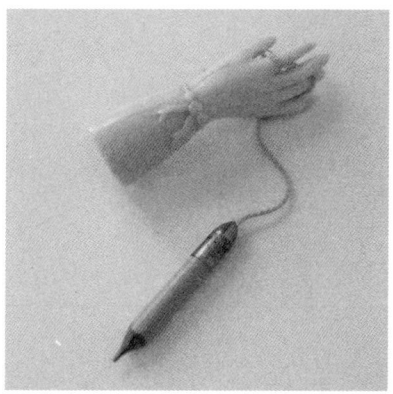

the sentence is sexy

it says 'Lovemelovemeloveme'
in a red dress & Elle McPherson knickers

you find yourself taking it seriously

★

there is a word & a word & a word

at the end of the words
                              there is a gesture

★

it opens out   like an umbrella

St Francis with magnolia and birds

birds ruffle
in petals plum & ivory
bent back like salad spoons

as he lifts & lifts up his arms

in a shudder of enamelled light
the birds fling out like a net
tripping all that is seen & unseen

till his shoulders hurt

& his wrists drift down
in a soft reshuffle of wings
folding back to buds between blooms

& the whole tree thickens

St Francis meets three ladies: poverty in sackcloth, chastity in white silk, humility in scarlet

after a painting by Sassetta

he must choose,
touching with his finger
tip her finger tip

★

the women leap
out of their skins
with excitement

(for this split
second you can see
all six of them)

★

& it is Lady Poverty,
in her hand a crinkly
frond of rue maybe

if it is blue enough,
who turns her face
back down to him

her bare feet drifting
like the claws
of a canary

modo de volar

there are stranger
ways of flying
like Goya's spinning

women squat
with their fists clenched
in a brush drawing

bulls' eyes on the wall

in centuries and in villages
where the women bore most
of the weight of a constricted
life, some of them flew by night

on broomsticks or even lighter
vehicles, ears of wheat or pieces
of straw, before being codified
by the Inquisition

Steve has three little daughters
with rosy cheeks
& threshed out yellow hair

he covers their long limbs
sometimes with fibreglass
on strips of linen

he makes a cast
he reconstructs his daughters
without heads

they hunch in the bare branches
of an aluminium tree
& shake their shoulders

heading towards the antarctic

i.

Like a slow run in a nylon stocking
from loop to loop unhooking

like the crotchets in a Palestrina Mass,
you slip from Kyeburn to Hogburn to Swinburn

on the Pigroot, drawing a straight bow
through the island-shaped-like-a-cello.

You know very well that you are lonely.

ii.

In a dairy near Owaka, the button
bulletins dart like neon tetras: *I think*

you have mistaken me for someone who cares!
and *Never trust a naked bus driver!*

You put one with your name inside a bottle
you will never throw away.

You are afraid most of all, of being rescued.

iii.

At Thule, there is a chill when you enter
the room. You are angry but you call it sad.

'The Reverend Wholers had *a holesome and godlye
preservatyve againste Desperatio*,' says the barman

but that was a hundred years ago. The aurora
startles. You are after, rather, a true

lotus harvest. You bring back lots of pictures.

anorexia

these are the acts of power
to give birth   to kill

you have a new notion

★

in a monochrome of beige sheep & paddocks
you try to say your unclear thing

you curl up like a wild rabbit

★

living out now in the open
you are the original food

drawing a conclusion on a paper dart

such is the language   you wash & cut
of exigency   & core yellow pears

                                              you could do
                                              with a pig

white & cool   the lawn is
as ointment   littered with them

english (room 202)
and three other points of view

i.

There are three fir trees *en face*
stroking the soft air.
The sky surprises.
The toilets are located, the paper is thick
& white & longer than any so far.
On the dark
stairs at the end of the lino, the departments
run over: Latin into Maori into History
into Linguistics.
It is vulgar to be surprised,
angling your knees in a tight skirt under a Staff
Club picnic table.
'I'd never have an affair,'
says Josh, 'with any woman over 45. By the time
you got her the way you wanted her,
she'd up & die!'

ii.

'My womb is big enough for two,' says Ruth.
'A double ensuite.'
                              If she'd had the baby,
she'd've lost the student allowance.
If she'd stayed with the father, how could
he've supported her & through her studies
on 50 bucks a week?
                              She'd gone to Lyndhurst
on her own, through the placards of the SPUC
men & women.
                              'They tell you all lies, you know,'
she said. 'They are infected by religion.'

iii.

Anastasia is abrupt & breathless.
She has to fly.
I have disappointed her in a huge way.
Like George Sand, she writes & writes
& writes all night.
                              She falls in love
with beautiful, helpless, younger men
in need of mothering. They ring each other up
from island to island.
                              It's quite hysterical!
She pushes the top knot of her straw hair
up into a wave & pulls it down again. Drags
thick black lines through computer pages
in a rage.
                              She wants to rewrite my whole life.

miriama

i.

On crossing the border, I always
change my name. A simple precaution
& you to guard my back
                    Maheno, Monte
Cristo, Waianakarua, Mt Misery & all
the wildflowers
                    I am heavy with loot
& disappointment, heading south again
down the soft underbelly of the island,
shedding skins
                    like coke cans on the Kilmog
& already the rain.

ii.

You are waiting, with or without
my blessing, in a blue room of pictures
torn from magazines:
                    Mother Teresa, Athena's
sandaled Victory, a sequoia forest, an avocado
pear, gazelles, two babies in a bath with a chimp,
Ayers Rock by sunset, Hare Krishnas
in their old gold, mud pools, a street kid.
                                        You have
a bruise on your cheek.

iii.

'Sit down & I'll tell you a story.

At Moeraki in the old days lived a prophet,
Kiri Mahi Nahina, who taught all the people
that Tiki had made them, not Io.
                              Te Wera, the warrior,
struck him down with his taiaha. Plugged his eyes,
ears, nose, mouth, anus with moss to contain
the heresy. Then he & his warriors ate him.'

iv.

Nothing is high, nothing is low, nothing
is hidden.
              This is the song, Miriama, you sing,
doublestopping on my heart strings.

the persistent levitator

There are too many words
like in a Russian novel

& easy to lose
the first ecstatic jolt

I trace with my finger
the fire-line of the volcano

I am undermined by your sweetness

★

The women are rising up
& down the coast from Kaikoura

spinning
            like turnips
                        out over the sea

The sun glints
off the steel caps of their boots

They are happy

★

Needing a word
for the little jumps
on the surface of things

(that certain
blurring of the edges
like the sea's turning back
or the gulls hitched up on elastic)

I'm still hanging around

My sleeves ripple like flags

party tricks

for Jules

it pays
to have a party
trick or two
tucked up
your sleeve
like Patrick's
pavlovas
or his blood
red T-shirt
with the white
blazon BETRAYAL
& you did brush
out your long
blonde hair
for that boy
(I know, I know
he was a real dick)
& people did stare
at the pair
of you &
an American said
in a big voice
outside Le Café
in Worcester
Boulevard
'My god, boy,
you look just like
Tom Cruise!'
which was true
& the police
bugged our house

you said
because he was
dealing but
nothing can go
too wrong
I say
for a girl
who can raise
one scathing
black eyebrow
higher than
the other
& talk
like Donald Duck

delicious as apples

'I'm taking the Teaspoon
Club to Mt Cook,'
says the bus driver

leaning on
the crystalline
perfection of the fact

& the tiny ah delight
like an ice-cream sundae;

tripping
at the same time
(this is always his intention)

into a new deliciousness
his difficult wife.

from

still
talking

ancestral voices and I'm listening

we're doin' alright
in this little land
we stole from the Maoris

ancestral Irish voices
raw, self-mocking, tough

when things got rough
they didn't make a song
and dance of it

they laughed, got drunk,
they called a spade
a spade and when I wanted

praise, *why, you're the girl*
your mother forgot to drown
was good enough.

the stories

Once upon a time
there was a little girl
in a flannel petticoat

who kicked up her heels
in her auntie's pub
where there was a well

in the middle of the bar
and you had to be careful
or you'd fall right in. A tomboy.

And the goat chased her
and she had to hide in the dunny,
hanging on like grim death

to the little string
that pulled the door back in.
Now there's the whinge

of the gate hinge
and your slow shuffle
through the garden,

dragging another bag
of cherry leaves. Your room
is full of plastic ivy.

Remember how we used to walk
crooked down Montgomery Avenue
to Benediction on a Sunday night

and you'd bump me giggly
into the soft bat wings
of the new holly?

These are our stories,
mother, and we'll stick to them.
Getting them straight.

from tomahawk sonnets

i.

So, I have done faithfully the last task,
digging into the sand at Anderson's Bay
where your sweetheart is buried.
And in that little beige chamber, cool,
ridged from the trowel, I have faithfully
placed the shocking weight of you, now ash,
in an elegant olive green box. Stroking down
the surface like a sheet. So, sheeted, sleep,
the sea at your feet where you swam a stylish
side-stroke once while on his back he bobbled
like a seal, potato toes held high'n'dry
above the waterline. *I have always loved*
big men. Leaving the water to rise and well,
the weight of it, I weep white berries.

ii.

The bones in my cheeks, a haggard mask,
the purity of grief. And they all wash back,
the deaths. The child sobbing rigid in her bed,
her need to touch just once again the wishbone
of the rabbit in his hot skin. How he'd drum
a warning with his big back foot of danger
in the street *when Aedh played his fatal harp.*
I was standing one day, you wouldn't believe it,
right there in the garden, pegging steaming
socks on the line (yellow hips on the roses,
white fur frost on the shed) when I fell,
just like Alice, right through the earth's dark
crust, no kidding, up to my knees in a perfectly
round tunnel he'd dug. A final kindness.

iii.

I've gone with you as far as I can in my replica
body. In Australia last century, an aborigine,
I'd've gone even further in a seven pound white
clay cap and gashed my thigh, shark rip,
to stand beside you in the doorway. How will I sustain
the loss of your disapproval? With a tricky lilt
in Ogham script? With combat breathing? Hey,
I'm the kid out on a limb in the King Tree
with twists of dates'n'cheese in greaseproof paper,
watching the big boys run on the bridge railing,
smoke fuchsia bark and curse policemen.
Waiting for you to call me in.
May Mary and Persephone spring the silence locked
upon your lips, the final, lovely shape of it.

iv.

To counter my *cleverness* gifts in your own tongue:
the shimmy you'd warm on the candles of the gas heater
(from the Latin, camisia, through Old French, chemise,
a little undershirt with rubber buttons); a meagre
slice of pleasure was *the size of Father Brown*;
and *we all have our own cross to bear.*
So here we are in Rosie O'Grady's bar
and the boozers bang their jars on the wooden tables
weeping, 'I wish I was back home in Derry' who'd never
I swear, even been there in the first place!
It's a great life if you don't weaken. No gapers,
no gawpers, no church, no priest. We knew what you didn't
want and had to make up the rest. Some bastard
unbrave, has already stolen the flowers from your grave.

v.

So, it's all over bar the shouting
and now you've gone jaunting with my blitzkrieg aunt,
your older sister, holed up for years in a shack
with her fat orange cat. A dab hand at scones,
finally she set her jaw, refusing even water.
There's still a few photos to go through. You
at eight *loved deeply darklier understood*
straight-back dancing at the Ceilidh, long dark
hair way past your bum, bellissima;
at thirteen reading in the Kaiapoi garden,
of Deidre maybe, one of the three sad stories
of Ireland. *If you write about me, I'll come back*
to haunt you. Look, it's no wonder I keep on losing
and finding and losing my place in the book!

vi.

The hills tonight are jaunty with lights,
the ETA chip truck more lovely than a circus.
It's nine months now, a womb-time,
and I'm hanging onto a jersey for the smell
of you (a cunning trick, milord!) appalled
that love should've left you in the firing line.
'God save King Billy!' 'God bless the Pope!'
Fight, you buggers, I hate peace!
The nanas softened after I was born.
It was the end of the war. The train kept stopping
at Cromwell, at Clyde, the driver, the guards
all boozed out of their minds *let bygones*
be bygones forever. You worried that I might arrive
before we got back home to Alexandra.

vii.

It gets harder and harder to get a grip on all
this. Even the big houses are shifting,
here today and gone tomorrow, cut
in half, jacked up on a truck (the speculators
happy as a box of fluffy ducks) and carted
off to the country. Stripped to the waist, the builders
are making a sound-house 'I hear you call
my name' (Madonna) all tuned in
to the same FM. I've got to get
my tongue around it: politician, do-gooder,
safe-cracker, et cetera. Daughter.
Traitor. Daughter. *Actions speak louder*
than words and blood is thicker than water.
I'm still talking as you walk away.

x.

You called me Little Bear after the girl
who saw the Lady in the grotto, after
the movie. Oh, I am heavy with you,
shut down on a green seat on the hillside
above the Gardens, a duck alongside
cranking its little wooden clapper. See,
this is your crooked finger turning the pages
for me '*through light through dark*
the journey is alternate' – soft madrigal
of the blue gentian – '*we are privileged*
in our sweet skins.' Airy, my heart lifts,
drifting down the aisles of the blue cathedral,
listening for the music, shifting the blue furniture.

poem in the matukituki valley

I know some things
like you'd rather have seen a rotary
clothesline in my garden than roses

and when I dedicated my book of poems
to you, you hammed it up, mock horror,
with 'Jesus, what next!'

So coming down from the mountains
when Rae asked me what you would have thought
of it all, the grandeur, the excess,

the jade water, the yellow starred flats,
the black peaks with snow like orca leaping,
I had to say that I didn't have a clue,

perhaps something like *what a fuss about nothing!*

and now at night, as the comet works its way
across the greybright sky, I see no sign
that you like Caesar have become a god,

you are far too reliable to be a god,

but rather the gauzy face of a woman,
hair streaming, running with a baby in her arms,
saving me again and again from the burning house.

duck

there's a duck on the road
its head sticking out of the shiny dark
twisting like a tap turned on turned off
it's hurt, it's stuck
on the thin white line that divides
four lanes of manic traffic

why did the duck cross the road?
because she thought she had to
because her mother had done it before
because she didn't think she had to think
because she was hungry

onoff onoff onoff

consider for a moment
the domestic situation of the duck:
the rough nip on the neck the bluster
the headshove under water
the fluster and wing flap indignant
the flash of an indigo armband

why did she fall for it this time?
the fat wibble wobble of a batty criss cross trundle
on the Main South Road, ten little Speights babies
left tweedling on the thick brown skin of the river

she didn't know / oh yes she did
oh no she didn't / too right she did
she knew damned well and she should have known better

onoff onoff onoff

someone's got to do something
oh yeah! she's made her bed and now she'll have to lie in it
you'd be far better off to whack her on the head
and put her out of her misery
just how much can you afford to invest in a duck anyway?

this is a classic film noir
one of us is the femme fatale
one is the chap's best friend
I just wish I could remember the ending!

I'm a gymnast on a narrow beam
I ride the slipstream of hot metal
it's wet, the road is slippery
people are in a hurry to get home
I'm a collapsing Z

I grab the duck

      the twiggy cretonne feathers scissorslip
      a bit I dig harder into her hot gut the way
      I would if I was stuffing her before basting

I wrench her off the road

      dumb demure dappling   her neck wobbling
      away from me   her open beak   her dribble

I hold up the duck like a trophy

WOMAN KILLED IN RUSH HOUR TRAFFIC
SHE WAS TAKING HER LIFE IN HER HANDS
SHE WAS HOLDING A DUCK IN HER HANDS
SHE WAS OLD ENOUGH TO KNOW BETTER

all the way home I crash the gears crying
and I rush into the house to get a blanket
and the others say what's wrong
and I say I've got a runover duck in the car
and I need a blanket and they all start to laugh
and make helpful suggestions like

it won't make any difference
I've got more to worry about than a bloody duck
it'll be dead by now anyway and there's no room
left in the garden to bury things, god almighty,
we've already got two dogs, three mice, five goldfish
and the rabbit buried there, what more do you want?

and they're right of course
when I go back out to bring her in
she's dead

aue! aue! what will I do with you, *my own aisling?*

Queen of Spades in a brown tweed coat,
rock skimmer in scungy water, corky decoy,
topsy turvy lady of dibble and dabble, mud shoveller,
funny puddler, silly quack quack

shaddai

for Joanna Margaret Paul

'Could the fullness of humanity ever
have happened within the confines of The Garden?'
I'm reading to Joanna, backed into a gate
at Seacliff. Rusty padlock, rusty chain,
the land falling away. The asylum is empty.
We've eaten pickled walnuts on ryebread
and brie and now she's painting the beautiful
big blue sea, her left hand
open on her thin knee. 'Did you know,
my dear, that Shaddai, the Breasted One,
is one of the many names of God in Genesis?
That the other name for Eve is Zoë, Life?
That Isaiah's prophetic poetry
was written, more than likely, by his wife?'

a vision at warrington beach

for Sandra Winton

We are such old
friends, one hundred
years equal between us,

standing on the edge
of the sea rocking weed.

My narrow feet
are barred brown by sun
through my sandals,

the left foot slightly
longer than the right,

the right ear slightly
lower than the left

and a tiny barb
from a dentist's probe
broken off in my jaw.

I tell you these things
so you will recognise
the body.

You say you have passed
through the bleeding,
it has all stopped
for you and for a year

and we throw up our arms
and cheer and I say, well,
I might just start
a baby, *jesus!*

and we crack up
and fall about laughing
in the sucking swell,

more than half in love
the both of us,

with that big, fat woman
flapping her arms
in a floral tent dress ·

and especially
her strong, thick ankles.

song

stone woman, stone woman,
squatting on the grass
in front of the doctor's rooms

the red leaf, the yellow leaf falling

one big knee up behind your head
like a wing, and one big arm,
one big nipple in the mouth
of your square-headed baby,

stone woman, stone woman
I'm heading to work

the red leaf, the yellow leaf falling

I'm staring from the belly
of my Japanese car as this little kid
in a raggy T-shirt and track pants
from St Vinnie de P rolled up

the red leaf, the yellow leaf falling

clambers into your big stone lap
and sucks on the other one, cold
comfort, stone woman

the room in the rain

for Gail Tatham

flickery light in the shallows
winged tremor of liquidamber
weedflowers in Cassandra's blue jar

'with much love' a postcard
of the Beatles from London, from Dublin
a rosary, beads like boiled barley

the big white desk

there are words I have to open here
like windows onto the wet verandah:
home for instance, and *husband* and *candour.*

lovesong

for JR

missing you
like I've been hit
and missing you
for years

in a doorway
somewhere between
the kitchen
and the laundry

missing the way
you tell me every day
I'm beautiful

putting a kiss
on my forehead
when I'm sick

and on my tongue
a sweet exotic tincture
with your tongue

we could call it
ha–ka–ta–ra–me–a

picnic at hinden

another one for JR

We came here years ago,
remember. We stood
in lines with all the others

throwing eggs across
zigzag like bootlaces
taking one step backwards

every time. The day was fat
and glassy like a paperweight.
Surprise and no surprise

to find inside it then
a yellow cow, after Chagall,
a red bird, blue flowers,

a woman folding her arms
around a man and vice versa,
he lifting her up.

from

settler
dreaming

the leaving

so, it's time to change your point
of view   you'll sell up

start again   sick of all the old
stuff   even the huge cement

shell your friend made from a mould
shaped like a cabbage   the veins

and slender wiring inside painted
dark green   you're off

to make a go of it in Brisbane

★

open your mouth
mon petit chou
and tiny single

flowers float out
and turn slowly

showing their dark
like gullies caught
in red velvet

curtains behind which
the windows are blue
with microscopic

creatures etched in
this weta for example
her exquisite stretch

★

you leave the country
or rather the country leaves

you or rather you lose sight
of it or rather you lose sight

of yourself

                    for just a moment

all the family gathered and
pooling like water at the end

of the road and this one lifting
slowly his blessing hand

early settler

you dream a hand
        that will stitch a flag
to the bullet-hole
        in your shoulder

you dream a man
        who wears a huia feather,
stands all Heathcliff
        in the doorway
of the prefabricated house

you dream a door-post
        painted with your insignia:
a monkey, a black swan feather,
        a bike lock

singalong

so,
you thought you'd be set up
in next to no time

au contraire,
'the new land' continues to elude
like blue-eyed eels in the river

'the new land' ripens
like a bridegroom, like a bride

you take her in, you place
your hand on his murdered flesh
you are full of murmurs

★

you want to take her home
you want to keep her warm

you want to sit her down
by the fire
of bombed out cities

lying on the marble floor,
playing the didjeridoo,

she will be able to be
your little acclimatised owl

tu whit tu whoo!

★

this is the song
        of your original sins:

the albatross around your neck
            the botched document

hello, kia ora!
this is a message from New Zealand!

waitara canticle

Someone has dug with a patu
a ditch in the sunlit meadow
of her wide forehead. See

the ashy Lenten cross
she delights in wearing,
the shark-toothed necklace.

Her tongue extends, a sacred
vessel. She opens her dark
throat and there's this odd

singing of the air as it moves
through the clerestory, a white
flume. She is surprisingly

sturdy as the wood pigeon
within the smooth musculature
of the Atlas Cedar is sturdy.

She's Cheryl Moana
Marie, loosening her queenly
fretted throat and tiny

silver birds fly out,
their breasts plumping
as they swing ceremoniously up

and down and open
the little hinged gates
of their silver beaks; and tiny

silver keys fling out,
the neat nick where each one
fits into its lock,

all the mechanical parts
and it's his and hers and ours
and theirs and we say

hey, hang on a minute,
we'd better all listen
this time, don't you reckon!

famine

i.

A slate step, a brass knocker, the old
forgotten greeting, *faílte*. I thought the stories
were a true map of the landscape by which
I might remember how to read the tribal colours
painted on the lamp-posts, the pinched face
of the man on the bottom rung. It was strange how much
Strabane was like the Taieri, that one black
headstone out on its own, 'The burying ground
of the Colhouns!' And at that very moment
the wild geese flew over, two strings of them,
one from the right hand side of my head and one
from the left, cleft whakapapa. And that's when I
remembered what Cassandra said as I was leaving,
'You will find your own famine in Ireland.'

ii.

My mother's great-great-grandfather strikes
my father's great-great-grandfather in the face
with his fist and my father's great-grandfather
stabs my mother's great-grandfather in the chest
with a pitchfork. Broken harvest.
Then my mother's favourite uncle lays about
my father's favourite uncle with a club, we
womenfolk screaming for blood as he pushes
his head down under the water. I have added
my stone to the stones of the others, casting
them down from the bridge. Then I washed
my hands, thank God, of the lot of them,
stole the family horse and on the proceeds,
took my message of peace way down to the Antipodes.

iii.

There are flockings across the continent, thousands
of hawks, and here I am with my face uplifted
in Coralville, standing next to Suchen
in the middle of the street in the middle of the wide
Midwest, the heavy, slow-spoken pilgrims
plodding past to McDonald's. When they ask me
to establish *home*, I conjure two Paradise
ducks in a rough paddock, the hills lined up
like the backs of quiet animals. In the caves
behind the Mayflower, runaway slaves
hid out – *'If I harbour you, will you harbour
me?'* Sweet Honey in the Rock at the Hancher
Stadium. Chickasaw girl stomp-dancing in
Dubuque. There's never been a famine in Iowa.

cairn

Rusty knuckled iron remains,
the paddock cleared of stones.
Haft, shaft, bucket,
imperium, lode. His hand
on the language, hers on the hoe.

open field

The earth's cold sweat, white rime on the rectangular
field like beds of daisies, the moisture cool on your arms
like ointment and on your face; the trees standing around
patient as packhorses; the blue militia, the white hikoi.

Standing out in the open field, you slow your breathing,
you go deeper, blue swishes on the white sky, smooth
as the stone the little black poodle places on the polished
floor for you to throw thrillingly beyond her obsession.

The trees are heavy with green cloud, a tent you can walk
under and the light changes. You're taller, your skin opens
with little pricking sounds, up and down the airy ladder
the plucking of soft nests, like Chris's aeolian harp.

We are what we love and you love the way the painter fades
the body into the page so the paper itself becomes the skin.
The way she opens the head as you might open a field cleanly
with a spade, the sea streaming sideways like a Ugandan postmark.

sonnets for a sister

so busy

She writes: 'These are the scouring days.
I spend my time playing the piano, learning

Greek and baking bread for the Quakers to take
down to the land protesters camped on both

sides of the river. All the colour has gone
from my palette. I paint only the white sky

and the white sea while you, my dear, are so
so busy.' What a joke. Someone

should tell her that all I'm really doing here
is sitting weirdly on a little chair in the front

window of the BNZ, Riccarton,
counting money. It's an advertising stunt. It pays

the bills. Out front there's this bored-out-of-your-brain-type
security guard, yawns, scratches his balls.

honest to god

She made an oath in Tijuana to tell the truth,
honest to God, about love. This was a change.

She pulled apart an orange, gave a fibrous slice
gold and white to a worn-out madonna

mumbling her lips in the Revolución
car park. Turquoise and silver earrings

sparked on cards in the darker doorways.
'Dear lady, stop. Will you marry me

please?' said the alcoholic son of the famous
sculptor. 'No. You are lovely indeed in your chaotic

shop but you've already told me you've got a wife
at home and six kids. I'd much rather buy

these Mickey Mouse socks and this odd little porcelain
duck with holes all over its back for toothpicks.'

be well, be humble

She writes: 'In the dream I am the victim
of a car crash or a domestic dispute,

you decide. I'm lying white in a white
bed in a white ward with little black

stitches like staples hitching ten red
slashes on my arms and my face,

when suddenly the stitches twitch, arch
and flick out. It's anacondas and

tarantulas. Scream.'
                    'Be well,
be humble,' says the whiskey priest

in a courtly fax on gilt-edged Papal paper,
'even as a tumble of runner beans on a compost

heap is humble. Anything other is vice.
How lovely to hear your new voice.'

dear swimmer

Like the little black poodle gulping
on the polished floor, she is desperate for even angry

company. The news is all of drownings in rivers
and car crashes; the sky plump and rosy

like beautiful Chinese mouths. 'My body,' she says,
'now expects pleasure and without the mirror

in the room sex is definitely safer.'
So. She disguises her disguise,

writing it appropriately in a collection of short
fiction. 'The map is not the territory,' writes

Alfred Korzbysky. Dear swimmer, you could
go crazy thinking about things like this.

Better by far to steer clear.
Help Tejinder sand down the old car.

go easy, sweetheart

Hydrangea clouds are loosed and floaty
on the black pool. She's making a hard job

of it, the little girl with the wooden spoon,
creaming the butter and the sugar. Go easy,

sweetheart. Little bubbles exploding soft
like years later when he licks and licks and little

bomb blasts like pain that must be entered
into, like delight. Her knuckles whiten,

her elbow is rigid with blessings: lavender shortbread
and honey ice-cream and all manner of berries.

I can only understand you when you speak with an American
accent. She's watched it all before – flower,

fruit and fall. Aha, so that's how it's done!
Still wondering how on earth it is to be done.

the murdered girl

from over near the beach the first bird stirrings
gold staples diagonal on the iron roof the streetlight
sets up steps a golden shop on the edge the trees
in gorgeous aisles she'll fly down the island in an old
Holden stand like a troubled angel wings outspread
against the war memorial look down over the city
a tabled expert the big bay window in triple brick
a glimpse through to the Peninsula the ivy wrapped
at night in soft grey cloths the stink of yellow bird-juice
from the smashed egg the glacier's stones are rising
through her head the mansion built in a day built in
a river bed the silly starling's three-note imitation
of a cellphone lower lip tucked under sour cherries

the icebox

for Graham Lindsay

The vodka bottles stick up
like ducks' necks out of the chillybin.
The ice has been mushed and refrozen like a coffin.

Trapped in ice walls, flowers
and leaves pluck the epileptic water.

This is what we call shipwreck.
This is what we call nightmare.

The circular drift of things still alive inside the ice.

sonnets for a brother

brrrm brrrm

You are braced. You are em-braced.
Your father was a very nice man

says your mum. In the dream you are running
past the dredge holes in the old gold diggings.

You are on the lookout for fathers. They keep on running
away from you over the green and gently falling

fields of Normandy or crash like drunks
onto the floor in a pub in Oamaru.

You are jumpy like a truck under a little boy's
hand brrrrm brrrm brrrrm in a sand

-pit. The Irish are all heart, the Dutch
are all head so you've had to live in Holland

for the last five years, to take a breather.
All that breathy talking and no closure.

a soft day

A soft day they say of it in Dublin,
just two hours away from the war. The women

in Baggott Street kneeling before the jewelled
doors of the tabernacle *let us lift up the bright*

tent of our constant voices. And at that very
moment the big man springs his big

red fist right into the side of your head.
You are flung up into the air, fall back

on your bed through the white doorway.
In much the same way, light strikes two

friends lying down side by side under
the gun. And all the while Marian sings

on, of Deidre's love for raven-haired Naisi;
of Lir's children saved, turned into swans.

yea or nay

You take a photo but it shrinks the blue
which shoots backwards away from you and no

face on the water. Let's face it, you are buying
time in Brisbane, yea or nay, travelling

hours every day in a water taxi,
reading comics. By mistake, you leave

your father's photo on the warm brown seat.
Sometimes I just do things like this.

Scars and a plastic dressing river-glitter
like a guillotine on your aristocratic neck.

You are stitched up like a sack of swedes with a big
curved needle, a Malayan bush-knife.

Plunging into the words as into a chill blue
lake, urgent displacement of an old panic.

boo

He writes, 'I am buying a last little
slice of cheesy light, living more

and more subtly in this world before
I enter the next. Every morning I take

my fingers walking up the child's arm
boo on the pale ridges of the hand-adzed

table. Be assured I still adore
the tui in the puriri tree, its coughing

fits, its elegant language; the way it stays
away in Lent, comes back on Good Friday.

I am, dear sister, as fragile as a china
teapot wrapped up in brown paper and posted.

Poised like a diver, I am in position.
Remember me and my brilliant intuition.'

sweet-kiss-on-the-mouth

They came to your funeral from the Forensic Unit,
in suits, their dreds tied back. They brought

the cards they'd made, with drawings of little square
houses with triangular rooves and rectangular doors,

pakeha houses with smoke coming out
the chimneys, curved paths, flowers in the garden,

Our Father's houses in heaven. And in rickety
printing THANKS BRO FOR EVERYTHING.

Cuffed, they walked up and put the cards
on the casket, paused, lowered their heads

and prayed. Your life was like a line
of railway carriages heading south, none

of the passengers introduced to each other
but each one blessed, Sweet-kiss-on-the-mouth.

the lay sister

The lay sister slides her hands
through holy water. Chops
onions, carrots, celery

in that order. Splits
blocks of wattle. Her hands
are fat on the axe handle.

'Good God,' says the Bishop,
slipping another smoke ring
round the crystalline throat

of the Portuguese sherry
decanter. 'That woman
would knock you down as good

as look at you!' The lay sister
is as rough as guts, speaks
Irish rather than English,

sleeps through the mission,
eats by herself in the kitchen.
Sometimes however

they do let her answer
the door and it's 'Excuse me,
Reverend Mother, there's

a piano in the parlour'
(that's the given code word
for a man) and she not able

to keep herself from laughing
then, imagining knocking
a fine old tune out of him.

the big nude

for Kirsten Morseth

Kirsten has painted a big nude,
arms up as she turns, charcoal
on brown paper, the same way

a tree turns as you walk past it,
showing off in winter its beautiful
bones like the bones of a hill

with the skin slipped back, the sailing
ships at anchor in the harbour,
the knocking waves like smocking

on the baby's dress, the thickening
rows of v's in the crisp fresh-apple
green, the soft pouch between

the white wings, the ivory shell
that scuds with glassy puffs onto
the beach, burst sachets of stars.

But it's not Aphrodite, nor Isis,
nor Astarte. More like the woman
from the local fish'n'chip shop,

the one who gave a flea in the ear
to the insurance agent who wanted her life,
the real estate agent who wanted her house,

the priest who wanted to hear her confession,
the poet who wanted to confound her
with his tedious sex life,

the Chairman of the Business Roundtable,
the Governor of the Reserve Bank,
Olivier Burl who delivered her babies,

Bradman Princk who delivers her milk
and that sweet old guy who's worked for years
at the Aranui service station.

the bomber pilot

Anzac Day. Cathedral Square. The crowd wrapped
up against the chill, faces upturned. The long
thin elegant spire seems to lean forward as flashes
of dark blue and indigo swirl, the dark so vivid
with the bright jettisoned.

how she loved to walk in the dark

They fly over in loose formation, foreshortened
in the weird breaking light. They lift in the navy
sheen their rich plumage. Gulls. They wheel,
the whole group sensing it, just a slight rocking
of the head to ascertain spatial perimeters.

The light shines reverential on their underbellies,
on the young fathers with shaved heads and rings
in their ears, their kids perched on their shoulders,
on the Army marching past, the Boy Scouts, the Boys'
Brigade, the veterans with red-veined cheeks.
On all the medals.

> *brings a lump to your throat, eh mate,*
> *just like the haka before the big match* ka mate
> ka mate *or when that girl with the yellow hair*
> *grabbed a guitar and sang, open throat, 'Flower*
> *of Scotland', and Mel Gibson, why now,*
> *he's your man, and we all bravehearts, eager*
> *to kick the shit out of some Englishman*

That's when I saw him, slightly built, not tall,
straight black eyebrows, slanting hazel eyes, Niall,
son of the ancient Kings of Ulster. He had his RAF
greatcoat on, his hands punched deep in the pockets.

'I knew it was you. You have your grandmother's
fierce chin.' And he grinned.
Just one of the wild Irish boys spoilt by their mothers.
Hellraisers, doing wheelies down on Caroline Bay,
falling out of their cars at high speed, and after a night
on the town, rolling up to Mass on Sunday morning
still drunk, getting the girls pregnant.

for years I was too afraid to go there
                              the room turning to ice

I told him what I knew about Montluçon, the striped
awnings pulled down over the footpath in the Boulevard
de Courtais, the cinema in the Avenue de la République.
'Everyone says it was a piece of cake. To bomb
the Dunlop tyre factory. So what went wrong?'

He was silent for too long.

'It was the night of the 15th, right, September 1943?
You were flying a Short Stirling Mk III with 4 Bristol
Hercules XVI motors and 8 Browning 303 machine guns.
There were 7 in the crew. You flew with 120 Stirlings,
369 Halifaxes and Lancasters, 5 B17s . . .'

'We . . . we looked like a swarm of bees . . .'

> *Pilots, for the most part, cannot write.*
> *Writers, for the most part, cannot fly.*
> *To fly and to be inarticulate, to pretend to be inarticulate,*
> *became, with rare exceptions, inseparable qualities.*

'So?'

'The ack-ack that night was brutal.
Buckets of it everywhere. It's not funny having
to "deliver the groceries" in those circumstances.'

'And?'

'And . . . and I saw the heavy bombs, the "cookies",
going down. Each explosion sent a shock wave through
the earth. The air stank of hot metal, sulphur and cordite.'

> *57 civilians were killed in the raid,*
> *among them, Danielle Laville, 9 months old;*
> *Wladislaw Plaazynski aged 9; Marie Lafaye aged 10,*
> *with her mother and her father; Jacqueline Chery aged 15 with*
> *her grandmother. 60 hospitalised. 90 injured,*
> *mostly French workers in the factory*

'I knew I'd caught a packet.'

> *'. . . another one twisting down to the ground*
> *in smoke and flames . . .*
>
> *Oh boy! Oh boy! Look at that! Oh boy!*
> *That was really grand! Oh boy.*
> *I've never seen anything as good as this.'*
>
> *(Charles Gardner BBC reporting live on the Battle of Britain)*

'There was no time to bale out.
Most of my instruments had gone haywire.
I remember particularly that my gyro was spinning
crazily and the artificial horizon had vanished
somewhere into the interior of the instrument panel.'

in the darkness there is no horizon

'I felt the familiar blackout symptoms come on,
first the light turning yellow,
                              then red,
                                        then slow darkness.'

the whole machine became enveloped in flames and pieces
        began to fly off . . . as it tumbled down into the canal
                it looked like a blazing waterfall

'The others all got back. After a show like that,
you find it hard to remember what happened.
Just a few incidents like illuminated lantern slides.'

'You were the hope of the family. They never got over it.'

I told him of the sisters dead, strangled by their silence,
their high Irish pride. 'I've had to fight against it,' I said,
striking a pose. 'The poems are my battlefield.'

her magpie fingers signing it out
                yaketty yak – too much bloody talk

'It's quite something,' and he grinned again,
'the gift of the gab. But what I wouldn't give for a beer.'
And that's where he left me, drifting through shining
rooms of rain, the other side of the Bridge of Remembrance.

the merino princess

Bless all gentle creatures like the lion
that comes up to you pad pad as you sit
under the one thorn tree in the savannah,
lays its big round head in your lap.

Bless the hills in the Lindis where they shear
up like the blades of the Iron Age plough
Odysseus might have used to turn the sand
in his plan to avoid the blood muster,
stopping short of his baby son, the last time
we see him soft-mouthed.

Bless the survivors of the plane crash
as they float out into Antarctic waters dyed
glorious by the aurora australis, a soft touch
on the shoulder, that is all that is left.
Bless the chill that squeezes the life out of us.

Bless the furrow.

Bless the male, bless the female fruit,
the red bush, the flame, the pale cup,
the embroidered prayer rug, the serpent
in the abandoned bell. Bless the secret
green flower, the circlet, the paper pansies
on the float. Bless the Merino Princess.

Bless the stubble of her shaven head.
I recognise her, sweet receptacle, in a maroon
hand-knitted cap, leaning on an ionic column
in the old art gallery. We don't speak
of the abortion but there is between us
the cautious kindness of the war wounded.

the bride

for Marcus & Ka Kwan

Here she is, the beautiful bride,
made out of black electrical wire,
moko on her chin, mad flowers
springing from her skull, the curve
of her spine as she bends towards him.

He can't keep his hands off her.

The footage contains no violence
or fiscal anxiety. Just a few strong
visuals: the luminous bride, the moonlit
lawn laid out for pétanque,

Vallejo's young man unwinding
the shawls of her difficult language. It's all
that he ever wanted to say about
the melismatic, the flowing, the flowering

(of Love as World Soul), profound
symphonia, liturgy of oracle and ecclesia;
she, his living breastplate.

wedding song

a duck in a gum tree
      a lamb on a swing
and is this not the strangest thing,
      to dance wifely, husbandly to sing

★

the old Lagonda tearooms
      blue lagoon ice-cream
seeds shaken in a silver sieve
      waxed paper in the cake tin

★

beside the lake of greeny-blue
      beside the lake of bluey-green
this surely is a wondrous thing
      to dance husbandly, wifely to sing

omakau

The beautiful long back
of the woman in the black
and white photograph.

The shoulder-blades
of shorn sheep, the way
the light gathers there

as they bend and eat.
Then all start walking
in the same direction.

notes

Heartwood was published in 1989 in the Caxton Press Poetry Series edited by Michael Harlow. Joanna Margaret Paul designed the book, which features six original drawings of hers on the cover and within the text.

of Elephants etc was published in 1990 by Simon Garrett, untold press. The cover and frontspiece drawings are by Joanna Margaret Paul. The book was designed by Lindsay Rabbit.

The Persistent Levitator was published in 1994 by Victoria University Press. The cover features an original painting for the book by Gregory O'Brien. *The Persistent Levitator* was shortlisted for the NZ Book Awards in 1995.

Still Talking was published in 1997 by Victoria University Press. The cover features the painting 'Sisters Communing' by Jacqueline Fahey.

Settler Dreaming was published in 2001 by Victoria University Press. The book design is by Kathryn Madill. The book features eight original drawings by her, on front and back covers and within the text. *Settler Dreaming* was shortlisted in the 2002 Spectrum Print Book Design Awards, and for the inaugural Tasmania Pacific Poetry Prize in 2003.

p. 12: *pansies*: My father, James Sproule Colquhoun Gilkison, died in 1962. *I had just come home from school and greeted him. He was stepping from the bath. I could see his big, pale, broken reflection in the opaque bathroom door. Then there was a crash. Next thing my mother was cradling him in her arms on the bathroom floor, calling his name. He died there. It was his heart. I was 16.*

p. 17: *amica*: I first met Joanna when we were both teaching at St Dominic's College in Dunedin in 1971. 'amica' is Latin for a woman friend.

p. 36: *modo de volar*: Stephen Clarke is a sculptor. I taught with him at Villa Maria College, Christchurch, from 1982 till 1995. The passage in italics is based on a paragraph from *Six Memos for the Next Millennium* by Italo Calvino.

p. 42: *english (room 202)*: In 1991 I was Writer in Residence at the University of Canterbury. I am very grateful to Patrick Evans for his friendship and support at that time and since.

p. 56: *tomahawk sonnets*: named after Tomahawk Beach near the Southern Cemetery in Dunedin. In 1996 I was the Robert Burns Fellow in Dunedin

My mother, Noeline Dore Niall Gilkison, lived with JR and me and our three children for 20 years. She died alone in 1995, during the night which was Christmas Eve. We had celebrated her 85th birthday during the day with no thought that her amazing life was about to end.

sonnet vi: My father was born in Strabane, County Tyrone, before the division of Ireland. His people were staunch Orangemen, who loved my mother deeply. My mother's family were Catholics from Dublin and Waterford. The stresses of the Irish situation were played out at my father's funeral when his brother would not enter our house because a Catholic priest was leading the ceremonies. I have written about these things in an essay 'The Good Child', published in *The Source of the Song: New Zealand Writers on Catholicism* (edited by Mark Williams, VUP, 1995). Joanna also has a lovely essay in that collection.

sonnet x: The words in italics are quotations from the poem 'Cadence', which I wrote in memory of my father.

p. 63: 'aisling' (Irish) is something like an angel; a sacred symbol of freedom dear to Irish nationalists. I am grateful to Isa Moynihan for these details.

p. 64: *shaddai*: references are to *Womanwisdom* by Miriam Therese Winter (Crossroad, 1991). The location for this poem is Seacliff. Joanna also spent 1996 in Dunedin.

p. 67: The stone woman statue is a sculpture by Llew Summers. It is in front of the Ilam Medical Centre, Memorial Avenue, Christchurch.

p. 68: During my Burns year in 1996, I lived with Gail Tatham who at that time was a lecturer in the Classics Department at Otago University.

p. 69: 'ha-ka-ta-ra-mea': the translation of the Maori is 'the place where we danced, swinging little owl-skin bags of perfume made from Spaniard grass.' Bill Manhire sent me an advertisement which picks up settler usage with an unforgettable rhyme: 'Come and have a beer in Hakataramea.'

p. 80: 'faílte' (Irish) means welcome. In late 1997, I represented New Zealand at the International Writers Community in Iowa City, USA. In 1998, on my way home, I went to Ireland.

p. 80: Cassandra Fusco is from Ireland; she is the arts and cultural studies editor of of *Takahe* magazine.

p. 81: Suchen Lim from Singapore was also part of the Iowa comunity.

p. 83: *open field*: A friend, the Christchurch composer Chris Cree Brown, constructed an Aeolian harp which was set up in the Christchurch Botanic Gardens.

p. 84: 'All the colour has gone from my palette' is a quotation from a conversation with Joanna. Kathryn Madill has recently used the words in a sculpture, a little Latin dictionary open at the letter L, covered in a thin wash of gesso. The words drift along the bottom of the double pages underneath a comfortable pale green teapot; a lovely continuing conversation between artists.

p. 90: The original icebox was created by Rosalind, Graham's partner, to celebrate his 40th birthday.

p. 91: *sonnets for a brother* are dedicated to my half-brother, Peter Reid, who died in 1998. Peter was ten years older than me. My mother was a brave Catholic divorcée and a single parent when she met my father.

p. 98: Kirsten Morseth, artist, lived with us for two years in Christchurch.

p. 100: *the bomber pilot*: The pilot is my mother's brother, Alexander William Niall. His log book is still in the family along with official correspondence relating to his death. His name is on the war memorial in Alexandra, Central Otago. Details of the raid on the Dunlop tyre factory have been written up as a PhD thesis by a French scholar, Claude Grimaud. I am extremely grateful to my mother's cousin, Ray Niall, for making this text available to me. Another useful source was *The Spitfire Log,* compiled by Peter Haining (Futura, 1985).

p. 105: *the bride*: Details in the first stanza arise from the work of the Maori artist Jacqueline Fraser.

p. 106: *wedding song* is a bit of a ring-in. It was not actually published in Settler Dreaming but was written for the marriage of our son, Johnny, to Karen Cush in Brisbane, June 2002. It was also read at the wedding of Joanna Margaret Paul and Peter Harrison in February 2003.

p. 107: *omakau*: a translation of the Maori might be 'the place where my treasure is to be found.'

acknowledgements

With thanks to Creative New Zealand who have supported the publication of my books. Most importantly they have provided essential writing time in supplying funding through the Fellowship at the University of Canterbury in 1991; my participation in the International Writing Community in Iowa, 1997; a writing grant in 1999; and an Antarctic Artists Fellowship, December 2004. Thanks also to Antarctic New Zealand who co-fund this particular award.

Special thanks to the University of Otago and the benefactors who make available the Robert Burns Fellowship which I held in 1996.

Thanks also to the editors who have placed many of these poems in magazines and anthologies over the years. And to the Christchurch *Press* and Easts Bookshop who in 2003 presented James Norcliffe and me with awards for our contributions to literature in the South Island.

Particular thanks to John Dickson for that seminal poetry workshop in Dunedin all those years ago. And to Simon Garrett who first published my work in his literary journal, *untold*, in 1985.

Thanks to Jenny Bornholdt, Victoria Broome, James Brown, Geoff Cochrane, Fiona Farrell, Michael Harlow, Dinah Hawken, Michele Leggott, Graham Lindsay, Bill Manhire, James Norcliffe, Gregory O'Brien and Elizabeth Smither for their fine example and encouragement, and especially for their friendship. Particular thanks to Fergus Barrowman and Victoria University Press for their continuing support.

Special thanks to Kathryn Madill who is the perfect reader of poetry.

With much love to Maggie, Kathryn and Sandra, my special sisters.

And as always, love to JR, to Johnny and Karen, to Nick and to Jules, my dream team.

Joanna Margaret Paul inspired me with her love, her conversation, her paintings and her own fine poems for more than 30 years. Her untimely death by drowning in May 2003 remains a devastating loss. I dedicate this book to her.

Bernadette Hall was born in Alexandra, Central Otago. In search of a similarly wide open living space, she and her husband, JR, have recently fled north from Christchurch, across the beautiful River Ashley loved by Ursula Bethell. Into the Hurunui. They now live in a community of 80 souls at Amberley Beach, three walking minutes from sea.

For many years, Bernadette Hall taught Latin and Classical Studies in a number of high schools, while writing part-time. Best known for her poetry, she is also an award-winning playwright, and has from time to time turned her hand to essays, short fiction and critical reviews. She is sought after as a performer of her work and as a teacher of creative writing. She also enjoys working as an editor, an example being the popular anthology of Canterbury poetry, *Big Sky,* in which she collaborated with Christchurch poet James Norcliffe. She has been in turn poetry editor for *Takahe* magazine and the Christchurch *Press.*

In December 2004, Bernadette Hall and the Dunedin artist Kathryn Madill will spend two weeks in Antarctica, sourcing material for their next collaboration, an Antarctic fable in a picture-book format.